SCHOLASTIC

writing gu

With interactive resources on CD-ROM

Explanation Texts

Terms and conditions

IMPORTANT – PERMITTED USE AND WARNINGS – READ CAREFULLY BEFORE USING

for ages

9–11

Huw Thomas

Credits

Author
Huw Thomas

Development Editors
Rachel Mackinnon and
Marion Archer

Assistant Editor
Alex Albrighton

Series Designer
Anna Oliwa

Designers
Paul Stockmans
and Liz Gilbert

Cover Illustration
Mark Oliver

Illustrations
Andy Miles

CD-ROM Development
CD-ROM developed in
association with Infuze Ltd

Designed using Adobe InDesign

Published by Scholastic Ltd,
Book End
Range Road
Witney
Oxfordshire
OX29 0YD

www.scholastic.co.uk

Printed by Bell & Bain

1 2 3 4 5 6 7 8 9 0 1 2 3 4 5 6 7 8 9

British Library Cataloguing-in-Publication Data
A catalogue record for this book is available from the British Library.

ISBN 978-1407-11252-7

CD-ROM Minimum specifications:

Windows 2000/XP/Vista   Mac OSX 10.4

Processor: 1 GHz   **RAM:** 512 MB   **Graphics card:** 32bit
Audio card: Yes   **CD-ROM drive speed:** 8x   **Hard disk space:** 200MB
Screen resolution: 800x600

Contents

Introduction: Explanation Texts

The *Writing Guides* series aims to inspire and motivate children as writers by using creative approaches. Each *Writing Guide* contains activities and photocopiable resources designed to develop children's understanding of a particular genre (for example, fairy stories). The activities are in line with the requirements of the National Curriculum and the recommendations in the *Primary Framework for Literacy*. The teacher resource books are accompanied by a CD-ROM containing a range of interactive activities and resources.

What's in the book?

The *Writing Guides* series provides a structured approach to developing children's writing. Each book is divided into four sections.

Section 1: Using good examples
Three text extracts are provided to explore the typical features of the genre.

Section 2: Developing writing
There are ten short, focussed writing tasks in this section. These are designed to develop children's ability to use the key features of the genre in their own writing. The teachers' notes explain the objective of each activity and provide guidance on delivery, including how to use the photocopiable pages and the materials on the CD-ROM.

Section 3: Writing
The three writing projects in this section require the children to produce an extended piece of writing using the key features of the genre.

Section 4: Review
This section consists of a 'Self review', 'Peer review' and 'Teacher review'. These can be used to evaluate how effectively the children have met the writing criteria for the genre.

What's on the CD-ROM?

The accompanying CD-ROM contains a range of motivating activities and resources. The activities can be used for independent work or can be used on an interactive whiteboard to enhance group teaching.
Each CD-ROM contains:

- three text extracts that illustrate the typical features of the genre
- interactive versions of selected photocopiable pages
- four photographs and an audio file to create imaginative contexts for writing
- a selection of writing templates and images which can be used to produce extended pieces of writing.

The interactive activities on the CD-ROM promote active learning and support a range of teaching approaches and learning styles. For example, drag and drop and sequencing activities will support kinaesthetic learners.

Talk for writing

Each *Writing Guide* uses the principles of 'Talk for writing' to support children's writing development by providing opportunities for them to rehearse ideas orally in preparation for writing. 'Talk for writing' is promoted using a variety of teaching strategies including discussions, questioning and drama activities (such as, developing imaginative dialogue – see *Fantasy Stories for Ages 9–11*).

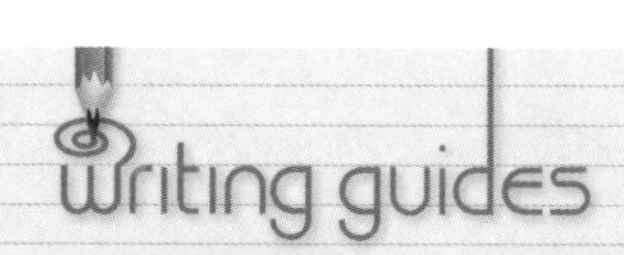

How to use the CD-ROM

Start screen: click on the 'Start' button to go to the main menu.

This section contains brief instructions on how to use the CD-ROM. For more detailed guidance, go to 'How to use the CD-ROM' on the start screen or click on the 'Help' button located in the top right-hand corner of the screen.

Installing the CD-ROM

Follow the instructions on the disk to install the CD-ROM onto your computer. Once the CD-ROM is installed, navigate to the program location and double click on the program icon to open it.

Main menu screen

Main menu

The main menu provides links to all of the writing activities and resources on the CD-ROM. Clicking on a button from the main

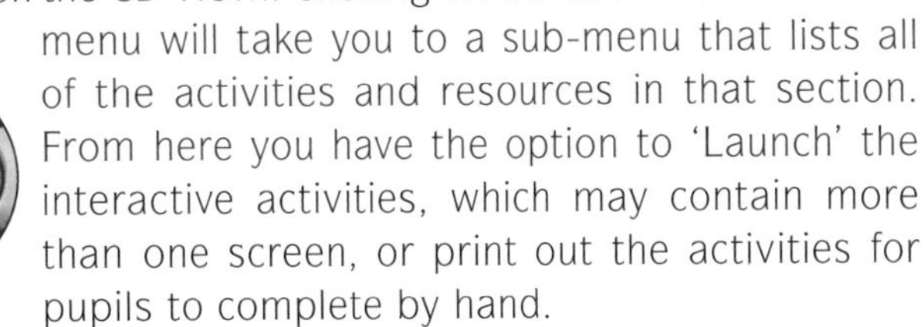

menu will take you to a sub-menu that lists all of the activities and resources in that section. From here you have the option to 'Launch' the interactive activities, which may contain more than one screen, or print out the activities for pupils to complete by hand.

If you wish to return to a previous menu, click the 'Menu' button in the top right-hand corner of the screen; this acts as a 'back' button.

Screen tools

A range of simple writing tools that can be used in all of the writing activities are contained in the toolbar at the bottom of the screen.

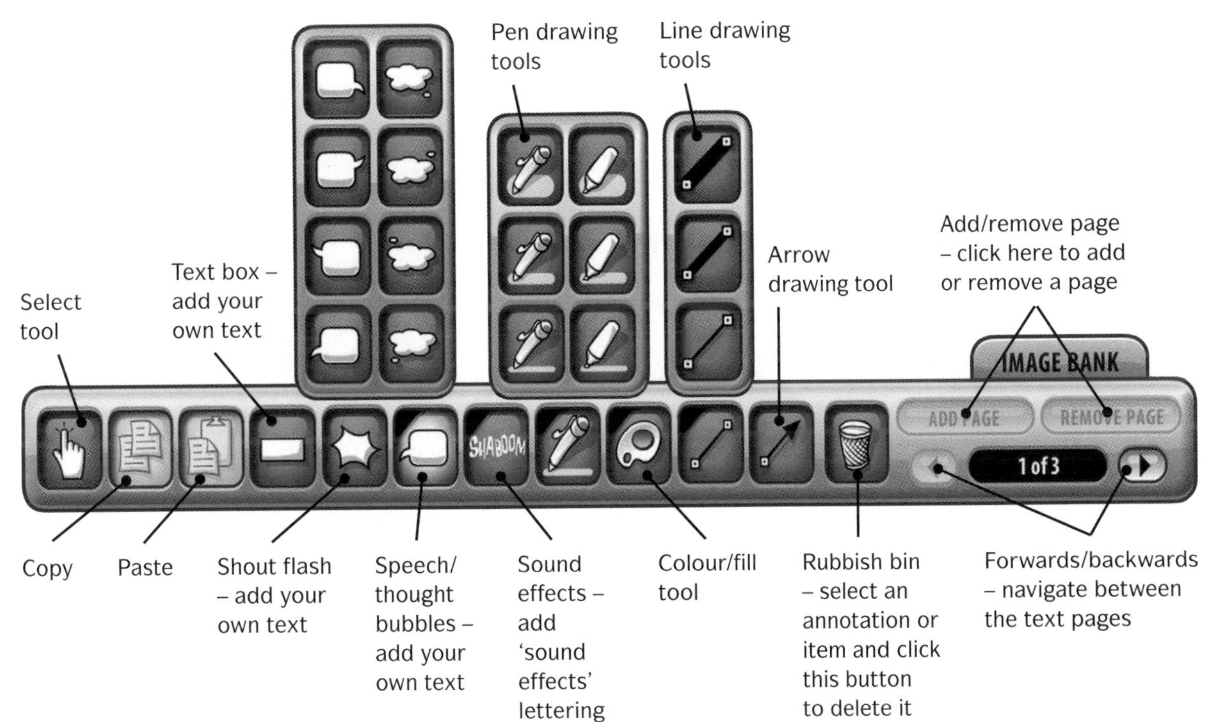

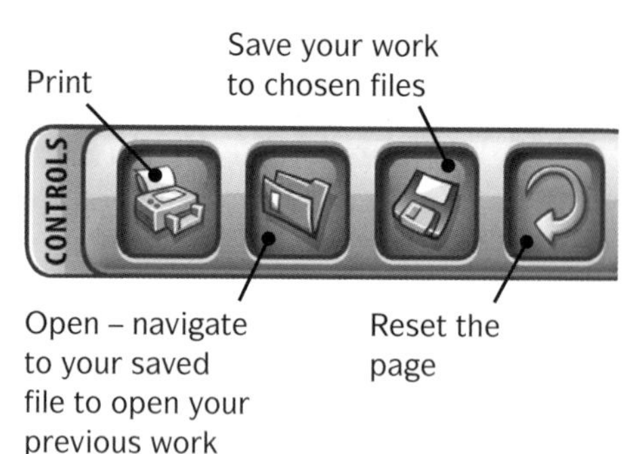

Printing and saving work

All of the resources on the CD-ROM are printable. You can also save and retrieve any annotations made on the writing activities. Click on the 'Controls' tab on the right-hand side of the screen to access the 'Print', 'Open', 'Save' and 'Reset screen' buttons.

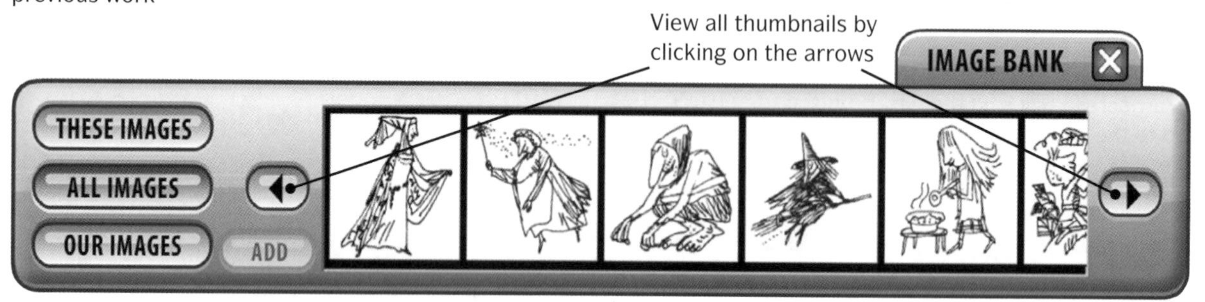

Image bank – click and drag an image to add it to an activity

Image bank

Each CD-ROM has an 'Image bank' containing images appropriate to the genre being taught. Click on the tab at the bottom right of the screen to open the 'Image bank'. On the left-hand side there are three large buttons.

- The 'These images' button will display only the images associated with the specific activity currently open.
- The 'All images' button will display all the photographs and illustrations available on the CD-ROM.
- The 'Our images' button will contain any images you or the children have added to the CD-ROM.

Press the left or right arrows to scroll through the images available. Select an image and drag and drop it into the desired location on the screen. If necessary, resize the image using the arrow icon that appears at the bottom right of the image.

You can upload images to the 'Image bank', including digital photographs or images drawn and scanned into the computer. Click on 'Our images' and then 'Add' to navigate to where the image is stored. A thumbnail picture will be added to the gallery.

Writing your own story

Each CD-ROM contains a selection of blank writing templates. The fiction genre templates will be categorised under the button 'My story' and the non-fiction templates will be categorised under 'My recount' or 'My writing'. The writing templates encourage the children to produce an extended piece of genre writing. They can also add images, speech bubbles and use other tools to enhance their work.

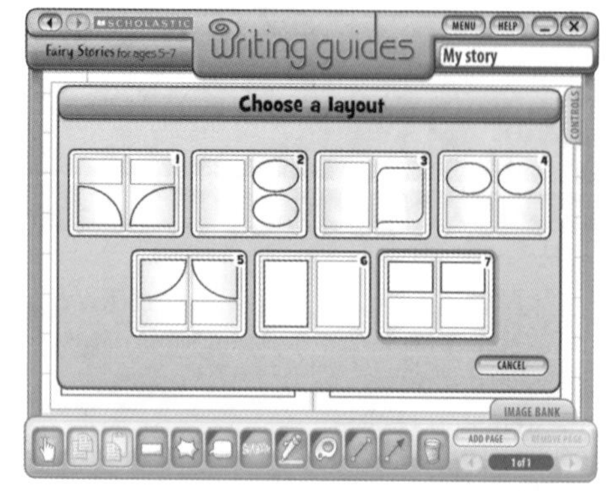

The fiction titles also include a cover template for the children to use. They can customise their cover by adding their own title, blurb and images.

Section 1

Using good examples

Explanation texts

To explain something, we say why or how it has happened. An explanation text is an account of a process. The aim is that we should understand its workings and possibly be better placed to apply that understanding – figuring out how a clock works enabled me, as a child, to repair one. An explanation text shows the steps in a process, one thing causing another, and so explains the outcome. It may refer to past events, the workings of social processes (such as elections), scientific models (such as the atom) or abstract concepts (such as forces).

The more interested children are in a process the better placed they will be to enthusiastically figure it out and explain it. In this section, a detailed explanation is given of a process that has a lot of interest for this age group and will support work on forces: the mechanism of a car engine. This example is supported by three shorter explanations that might appear as entries in a science encyclopedia. The idea here is to have a text that children will be using in their reference work, so they can get inside the structure.

It is important for the children to be aware that explanations are not just being about scientific and physical processes. They also feature in philosophy, sociology, the arts and politics. The final text works towards having some fun with the notion that something explained is understood, and understanding enables us to work with that process – in this case, the winning of a general election.

Links to the Primary Framework

Explanatory writing features in the Primary Framework for this age group, but more importantly given the shift towards cross-curricular themes, it has a vital role to play in a range of topics and is also a key type of writing for children to have grasped for secondary school.

The texts are primarily here as tools for learning how to write explanations. This means that the children should try to identify the content and style features of good explanations. They should be continually looking for how each text works, what they do and the way in which they help us to make sense of the world.

Explanation text features

Text
- Explain a process.
- Step-by-step structure.
- Introductory lines at start.

Language
- Time connectives for different steps.
- Causal connectives link one thing to another.
- Simple present tense.

Extract 1: How it works

What's on the CD-ROM

Media resources
- Discuss the image 'A car engine'.

How it works
- Text extract to read, discuss and annotate.

Techni-questions
- Roll over the questions to reveal information from the extract.

This extract uses a subject of interest to children to engage them in the workings of explanations.

- Before you read this text, display the image 'A car engine' from the CD-ROM and ask the children what they know about how engines work. Note what they say on the board, then ask them to list what they would like to know about the workings of a car.
- Open the extract from the CD-ROM and read it together, checking which of their questions have been answered.
- Annotate the text to show the use of technical vocabulary, circling any examples the children can pick out. Ask the children to re-read the text, looking for examples of one thing causing something, or something being caused by another thing. Find the words used to show these connections.
- Look at the diagram below the text and check how well it supports the explanation. Does it help to show the stages of the process?
- Hand out copies of photocopiable page 14 'Techni-questions'. Ask the children to cut out the questions and, in groups of six, take one each to research using this text.
- Using the interactive version of the activity, roll over the questions to display the text that answers it.

Extract 2: Encyclopedia entries

What's on the CD-ROM

Media resources
- Display and discuss the image 'Teeth'.

Encyclopedia entries
- Text extract to read, discuss and annotate.

Explain the word
- Drag and drop words to their meanings.

Encyclopedias are a mine of explanatory material, answering our questions about processes.

- Display the teeth image from the CD-ROM and ask the children what they know about the process of decay.
- Open the extract from the CD-ROM and look at the similar features of each text. Annotate the common features. (They all have the same function of answering a question; they give stages in a process leading to the outcome and they are written in the present tense.)
- A wave breaks, a boat floats and a tooth decays – but what stages make up each process? Ask the children to read each explanation and, in groups of three or four, divide the explanations into stages. Note how an explanation states the cause of something we observe by referring to previous events (such as a wave starting in mid-ocean), invisible things (such as bacteria) or abstract ideas (such as upthrust).
- Working in groups of two or three, ask the children to cut out and shuffle the cards on photocopiable page 15 'Explain the word', placing them in the centre of the group. Their task is to take turns picking up a word and explaining what it means. They can also complete 'Explain the word' on the CD-ROM.

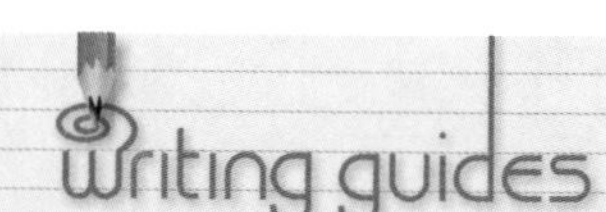

Extract 3: Elections

What's on the CD-ROM

Media resources
- Display and discuss the image 'Winning an election'.

Elections
- Text extract to read, discuss and edit.

This text gives an example of the explanation of a political process – one that many of the voters involved in it don't fully comprehend. Children may be entertained by the idea that explaining can give an insight into how something works – and who knows where that could lead!

- Before the lesson, ask the children to discuss the general election process with adults at home.
- Back at school, display the image of someone winning an election from the CD-ROM and ask the children what they have found out about the process. Open the extract from the CD-ROM and read it through together. Annotate the text to show what the children already knew and new information they have found out.
- Hand out copies of the extract and photocopiable page 16 'So you want to run the country'. Explain to the children that they are going to use what they have learned about the process to decide how the next government should be decided if they were in charge.
- Ask the children to work in small groups. As they work through the activity, prompt them to discuss the fact that children can't vote and look at who they could appeal to: the electors? Her Majesty?

Poster: Explanation writing

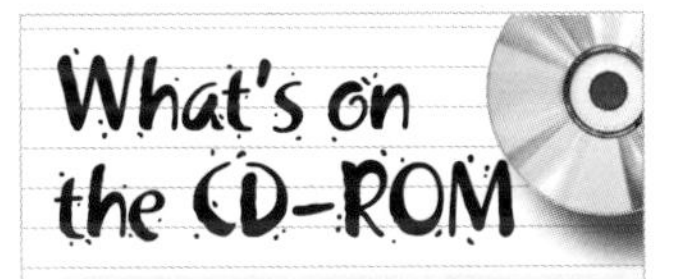

Explanation writing
- Roll over the features to see examples from the text extracts.

How it works, Encyclopedia entries, and Elections
- Text extracts to read, discuss and annotate.

We want the details!
- Roll over the text to reveal writing prompts.

The poster gives clear pointers on explanation writing, along with planning tips.

- Display the poster from the CD-ROM. Roll over the different elements to provide more information and read this together. The poster provides features the children have encountered in their shared reading to help them develop their own explanation writing.
- Using copies of the extracts, ask the children to annotate them when they find examples of a poster feature.
- The children could also use photocopiable page 17 'We want the details!'. Ask them to work with the poster and one card from the photocopiable sheet to expand the process. They can use the interactive version if they require prompts.
- As they progress through the writing of explanations, ask the children to keep referring to this poster. It can also be reduced to A5 and kept as a checklist in the cover of writing books, taken home for use with homework and so on.

Extract 1: How it works

A car engine is called an 'internal combustion engine' because the movement is caused by the combustion (burning) of fuel inside the engine.

The engine contains a set of cylinders. A valve at the top of each cylinder lets in a mixture of petrol and air known as a 'charge'. Once the charge is in the cylinder, a spark plug ignites it – causing a small explosion. This explosion pushes a piston down, pulling a weight attached to the piston upwards.

A second valve lets the burnt petrol and air mixture out of the cylinder, and the weight starts to push down. Consequently, the piston goes back up. Another charge enters the cylinder and ignites: down goes the piston, up goes the weight – then out blow the gases, down goes the weight and up goes the piston again.

A component called the distributor sends a spark to each cylinder at just the right time. Sometimes an engine needs tuning to make sure this works.

The piston is connected to a crankshaft. This has the effect of turning an up-and-down movement into a turning-round movement, a bit like a leg turning a pedal on a bike. The circular movement is then transmitted to the car's wheels – so the car moves.

All car engines have cylinders to burn the petrol and turn the crankshafts. Most have four cylinders, but some have six or more. The burnt gases leave the engine and are emitted from the exhaust at the back of the car.

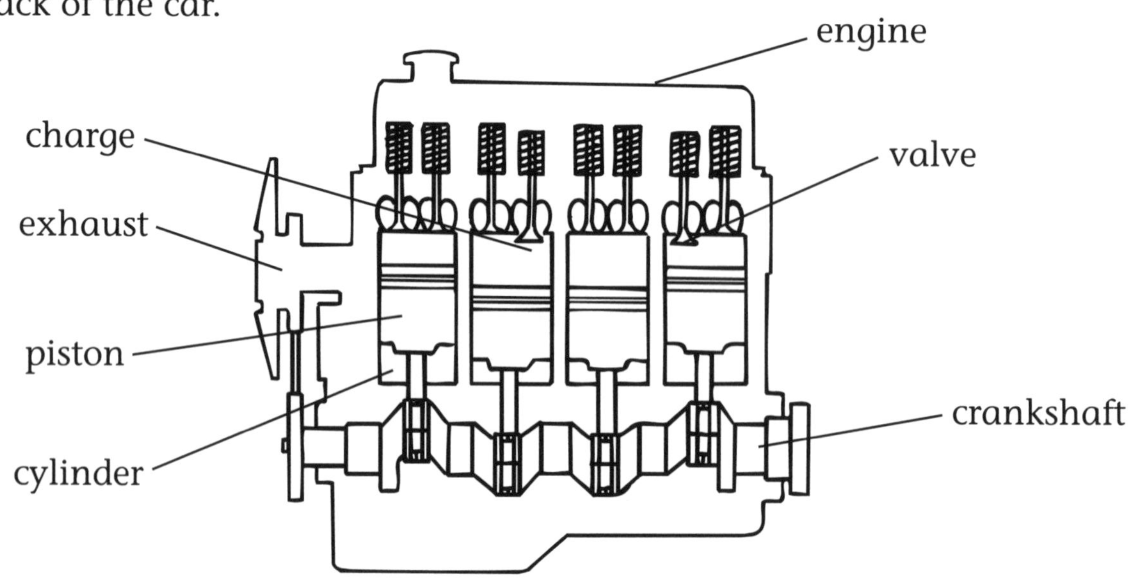

Extract 2: Encyclopedia entries

Why does a metal ship float?

A solid lump of metal will sink in water – but a ship whose body or hull is made from metal can float because it is hollow. The water pushes up on the ship with a force called upthrust. The bigger the surface in contact with the water, the bigger the upthrust. This is why ships are wide and flattened underneath. Because the inside of the ship is full of air, its total weight is not enough to overcome the upthrust – so the ship floats. If the bottom or keel were completely flat, the ship would float even better – but it would be much harder to steer.

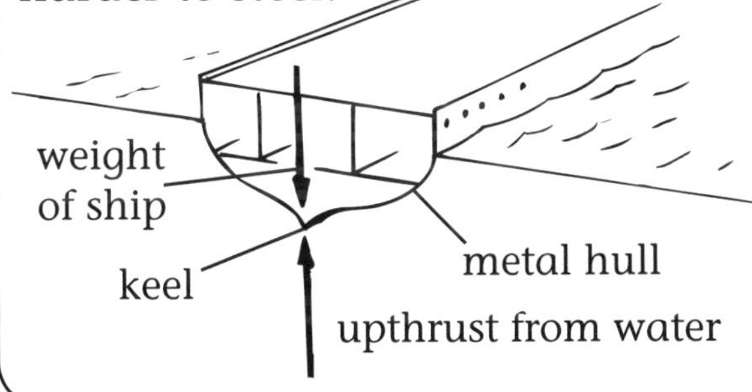

Why does the sea have waves?

Waves on the sea are caused by the wind. Inside a wave, the water particles go round in a spiral, like the cars in a roller-coaster. They become taller as the wind blows them across the sea. As they approach the shore, the water becomes shallower. The sea bed interferes with the spiral movement of the water particles, causing the waves to topple over or 'break' on the shore.

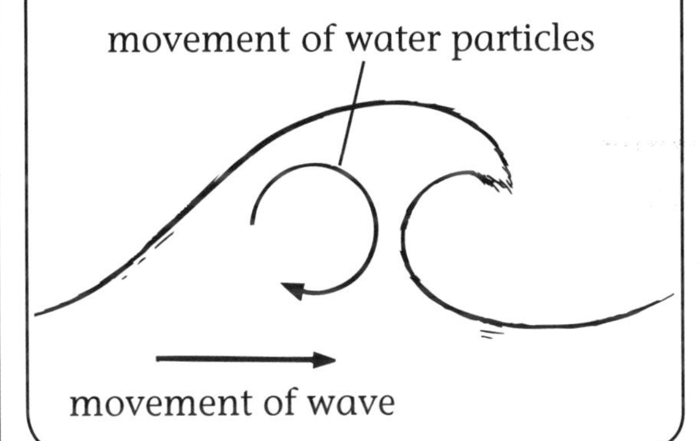

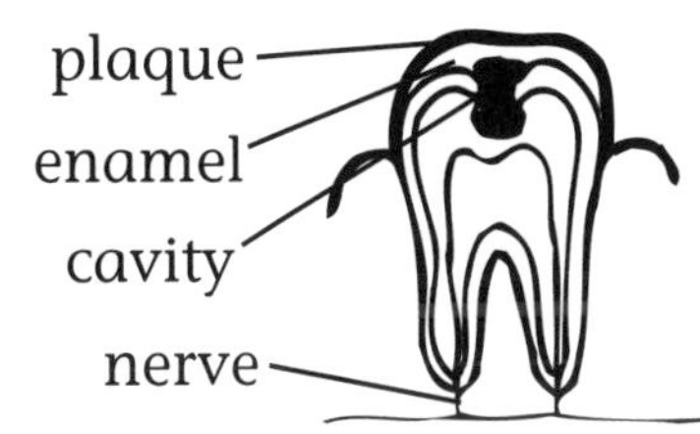

Why do we brush our teeth?

We brush our teeth to stop them decaying. Our teeth are protected by a hard layer called enamel. Fragments of food caught on the teeth form a sticky coating called plaque in which bacteria can breed – especially when the food contains sugar. The bacteria attack the enamel surface of the tooth and make a hole or cavity in the softer core, leading to tooth decay. When the decay reaches the nerves in the tooth, the pain starts! Regular brushing keeps plaque off our teeth and so keeps the enamel layer intact.

Extract 3: Elections

The United Kingdom is a democracy. This means the people get to choose their ruler (the word 'democracy' comes from the Greek meaning 'rule of the people'). So at least every five years, voters get to choose the new government. (Sorry kids – that's not you, because this country hasn't yet given the vote to children. Though that doesn't stop you petitioning for it!) You may be surprised to hear that voters don't actually vote for the prime minister. They vote for one of hundreds of members of parliament.

The process starts in each constituency – an area of the country containing a number of voters. These are large areas containing a section of the population.

What happens is that each one of these constituencies elects its own representative – Member of Parliament, or MP for short. An MP works for that constituency – they're the person you would write to if you wanted to see a change in the laws of the land.

For this to happen, in each constituency, a few people stand as candidates for this role, so they have to convince voters they have the best policies.

After a period of time, known as a campaign, the country reaches polling day. This is the day on which adults go and cast their votes. Later that night, in each area the votes are counted, resulting in the winning candidate becoming an MP.

By the early hours of the morning after an election the effect is that one party across the country could have more MPs than any other. This means that their leader will have support of a lot of MPs. In a way it's the MPs who then vote on the leader they want to run the country, though it is the Queen who has the final say on who should be her main Minister, or Prime Minister. She will call the winning leader to Buckingham Palace, asking them to form a new government. They decide the laws of the country – including the one that says kids can't vote.

The end result is a new Prime Minister and another five years before we all go through the same process again!

Techni-questions

• Here are some technical questions. Each of them requires you to explain something. Can you answer these questions?

How can petrol make pistons move?

What happens inside an engine cylinder?

What causes a piston in an engine to move?

Why do cars produce exhaust fumes?

Why are car engines called internal combustion engines?

How do the little explosions in an engine happen?

Explain the word

- Can you explain what each of these words means? Use the three encyclopedia entries to help you.

float	upthrust
decay	plaque
bacteria	enamel
interfere	hollow
particles	shallow

So you want to run the country

- Explanations can help you understand how processes work. That can be useful. Use the questions below to help your class decide how it could appoint the next government.

Who will decide the next government?

How will they decide it?

How old do you have to be to vote?

Could we do anything to change this?

How do we make someone an MP?

Where do we start?

Who do we need to persuade?

What should we do on polling day?

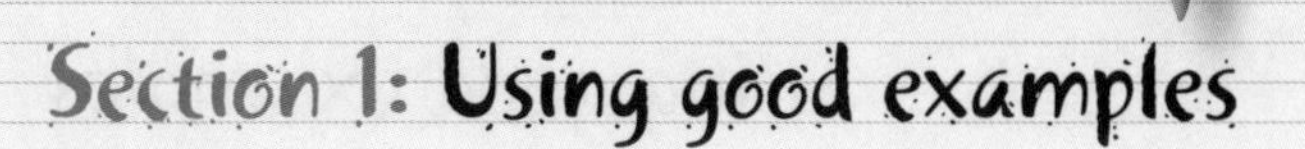

We want the details!

• These explanations are true, but they don't tell us very much. Can you develop them into fuller explanations?

Explanation writing

Remember...	**For example...**	**When planning, ask yourself...**
Show the **how** or **why** of something.	Why does a boat float on water?	What **how** or **why** question am I answering?
Describe a step-by-step process.	Charge ➜ spark ➜ explosion ➜ piston down ➜ weight lifted	What are the stages in this process?
Use time connectives for **when** each step happens.	'**Then** the tooth develops a cavity.'	Have I used words that describe a sequence in time?
Use causal connectives for **what** causes **what**.	'The shape of the boat **means** that...'	How did one thing cause another?
Use the simple present tense.	'Bacteria multiply...'	Is my writing set in the present?
Use technical vocabulary.	cylinder, piston, crankshaft	Have I used accurate terms?
Add a diagram if it will be helpful.	a diagram of a tooth	Will a diagram make the explanation clearer?

Section 2

Developing writing

Developing explanation text

Explanation writing takes a process and pieces together the steps in which it occurs, explaining how one thing leads to another. As such, the activities in this section build up the skills necessary to write such a text, with a specific focus on features highlighted in Section 1.

Children need a grasp of the process they are explaining – nothing is more frustrating for a child than trying to learn a complex genre while also struggling to marshal their information. In this section the emphasis is on showing the 'how' and 'why' of processes that are fairly familiar, either through day-to-day life (the tying of shoelaces) or subject matter they will have covered elsewhere in the curriculum (evaporation, sunrise). There is also a steer towards setting up processes for them to explain by doing things, such as lighting candles and melting chocolate. The basic point being that the more secure the process, the more children will enjoy applying it to the genre being learned. If gaining a grasp of this genre involves having a grasp of what is being explained, then the processes of questioning and researching are vital.

How to use the activities

This section contains activities that will prompt questioning and also looks at the use of KWL grids (what we know, what we want to find out and what we have learned) to define what needs to be found out about a process.

The activities offer ways in which the structuring of a process can be explored, with a particular focus on the connection of events by cause and effect, and the way one thing leads to another. This is translated into an exploration of the language used to connect sentences. As they do this, the children should be encouraged to gather causal and temporal connectives and to try using them. You will need to teach the connectives so that they find a natural place in the class's vocabulary.

The language of explanation is also explored through looking at the tense structure of two different jumbled texts and reassembling them, with a view to using the simple present tense in writing.

Activity breakdown

Concepts
- Arrows (page 20)
- Questioning (page 22)
- Planning and discussing (page 22)
- Chocolate changes (page 23)

Planning
- Planning and discussing (page 22)
- How and why KWL chart (page 23)

Text structure
- Cause and effect (page 20)
- Opening statements (page 21)
- Chocolate changes (page 23)
- Jumbled explanations (page 24)

Language features
- Link challenge (page 21)
- Pronoun hunt (page 24)

Activity 1: Arrows

Objective

To adapt non-narrative forms and styles to write factual texts.
(Year 5 Strand 9)

What's on the CD-ROM

Arrows
- Type the stages of a process into the flowchart.

What to do

This activity looks at how the recording of how one thing is caused by or follows another is a key aspect of explanation writing.

- Ask the children to look at how one thing leads to another in some well-known games. For example, the routine for 'Pass the parcel'.
- Open 'Arrows' from the CD-ROM and ask the children to think of any stage from one of your examples. Record the stage in one of the boxes, using note form. Point out that this can be from the start, end or middle of the workings of the game.
- Ask the children to then think of the other stages that make up an explanation of the process and add these to the flowchart.
- Complete the shared example before asking the children to try their own version using photocopiable page 25 or the version on the CD-ROM.
- Widen the discussion to include explanations of processes in technology (how something works) or science (outlining a natural process). Agree on a suitable process (such as the water cycle or the working of a fountain) for the children to explain using another copy of the photocopiable sheet.

Activity 2: Cause and effect

Objective

To experiment with the order of sections and paragraphs to achieve different effects.
(Year 5 Strand 10)

What's on the CD-ROM

Cause and effect
- Drag and drop the causes and effects to make complete sentences.

What to do

In this activity, the children investigate cause and effect statements.

- Open 'Cause and effect' from the CD-ROM. Ask the children to read the sentence parts, seeing if they can work out which cause matches which effect.
- Try matching some examples on the whiteboard, checking the right cause links to the right effect. Discuss which is which – what comes first and what follows as a result?
- Working in pairs, hand out copies of photocopiable page 26. Ask the children to cut out the cards and then shuffle them. They should then sort them into causes and effects. Can they fit the pairs together by identifying the process being explained in each sentence?
- Point out the connecting words used to start the 'effect' clauses. Ask the children to make a list of these words.
- Now ask the children to remove all the effects (the second clauses) and shuffle the causes (the first clauses). Ask them to read each cause and think of an effect in their own words, then write out the whole explanatory sentence. They can refer to their list of connective words to help them. Then they can rebuild the earlier sentences and compare these with their own versions.

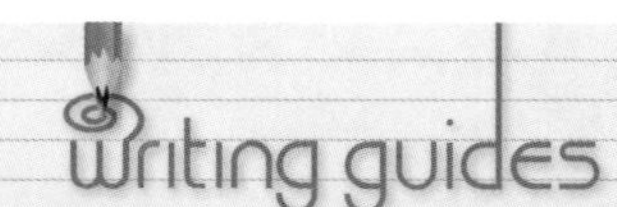

Activity 3: Link challenge

Objective

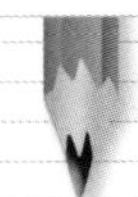

To express subtle distinctions of meaning, including hypothesis, speculation and supposition, by constructing sentences in varied ways.
(Year 6 Strand 11)

What's on the CD-ROM

Link challenge
- Drag and drop connectives into the spaces.
- Type a two-part sentence in the boxes.

What to do

The making of connections is central to the process of explanation. This activity supports the children in experimenting with the varied phrasings language offers such a task.

- Ask the children to work in groups of three, researching a topic that interests them and in which there is a process that can be explained, such as a magic trick or the extinction of the dinosaurs. You could provide some reference materials on specific subjects, such as machines or geographic processes.
- In their groups the children need to think of a connection that takes place in their area of interest.
- Open 'Link challenge' from the CD-ROM. Ask the children to look at the list of connectives available and select the one that best links the connection they have discussed. They can then drag and drop this into place and type the two-part sentence in the boxes either side.
- The challenge can be to use as many of the connectives as possible to create sentences about the process they have discussed. Note the major change between causal and temporal connectives. Then, within the causal connectives mark the different stages of cause and effect.
- Individually, ask the children to complete photocopiable page 27 'Link challenge', aiming to use all the connectives on the sheet.

Activity 4: Opening statements

Objective

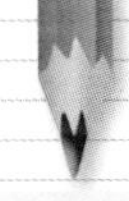

To establish, balance and maintain viewpoints in non-narrative texts.
(Year 6 Strand 9)

What to do

An explanation often begins with an opening statement that introduces the rest of the text by summarising what will be said. This activity supports the children in presenting these statements.

- Tell the children that, instead of writing explanations, they are just going to write first lines.
- Distribute copies of photocopiable page 28 'Opening statements'. Model how to complete the sheet. Think of a potential subject and record it in the first column. Ask the children to think of a 'how' or 'why' question they could answer about it. This can be recorded in the second column. Then think of an appropriate opening sentence that would introduce the topic in broad terms and record this in column three.
- The children can choose topics from their current work across the curriculum or from their own interests. For example, if they were explaining why spiders make webs, they could write: 'Spiders make complex webs to stay alive'.
- Remind the children to use verbs in the simple present tense ('make', 'get' and so on), indicating a process that is happening continually.

Activity 5: Questioning

Objective

To reflect independently and critically on their own writing and edit and improve it.
(Year 5 Strand 9)

What's on the CD-ROM

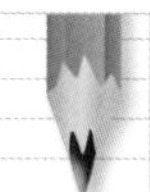

How it works
- Text extract to read and discuss.

What to do

Explanations answer questions. Creating the connections required for explanations involves devising good questions, which is what this activity focuses on.

- Hand out photocopiable page 29 'Questioning' and look at the phenomena described on the left-hand side. Point out the fact that some things will happen before and after each of these things and be connected to them.
- Ask the children to think of two questions they would like to ask about each fact. For example, for 'The Sun rises in the morning', the children might ask *Where does it come from?* or *Why does it rise?* Tell the children that they need to complete the photocopiable sheet, devising two questions about each fact. (You could refer the children to Extract 1 'How it works' for the final box.)
- When they have completed the sheet, organise the children into groups of four to six. In their groups, ask the children to decide which fact has provoked the most different questions. Ask them to write this fact on a large sheet of paper and write their questions around it. Discuss what explanations might answer these questions.

Activity 6: Planning and discussing

Objective

To set their own challenges to extend achievement and experience in writing.
(Year 6 Strand 9)

What's on the CD-ROM

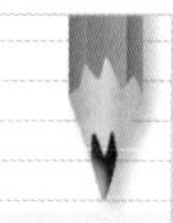

Planning and discussing
- Choose an image from 'These images'.
- Type notes to describe the process.

What to do

To explain a process, children need to muster some of the thoughts they have about them. This activity picks up on processes into which they should have some insights.

- Open 'Planning and discussing' from the CD-ROM and choose a process from 'These images'.
- Working in groups of three, ask the children what they can explain about the process. They do not need to do this step by step, they just need to come up with parts of the process.
- Ask the children to select a different process from 'These images' and, in a shared or guided session, draft some notes on the board.
- Once they have made notes on the screen, ask each group to cut out the question cards from a copy of photocopiable page 30, shuffle them and lay them out face down. In turn, they should pick up a card, then give a short, oral explanation. The other members of the group can help them along, but they need to try and explain the stages of the process and how they connect together.
- Once each member of the group has completed two explanations, they can choose one they would like to write as a short text.

Activity 7: Chocolate changes

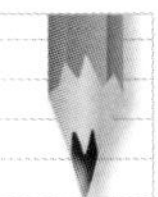

Objective

To change the order of material within a paragraph, moving the topic sentence.
(Year 5 Strand 10)

What's on the CD-ROM

Media resources

- Discuss the 'What happens when chocolate melts?' audio clip.

Chocolate changes

- Drag and drop the stages into the correct order.

What to do

This activity allows the children to observe something so that they are writing about things they have experienced.

- Before doing the writing activity, melt and cool a chocolate bar. Play the audio clip from the CD-ROM.
- Open 'Chocolate changes' from the CD-ROM. Can the children take the six events and place them in the order in which the process happens? Drag and drop the events into the correct sequence.
- Provide the children with photocopiable page 31. Ask them to cut out and sort the images in the correct order to explain the changes. When they have done this, encourage them to take time pointing to each image and saying to themselves or a partner what the main thing was that happened at that stage in the process.
- Point out that for each stage there is a main sentence – the main thing to say about that stage. Together, write a paragraph about the solid bar – possibly adding sentences about how it feels to touch. The main idea (the bar being solid) could come at the start or after some description. Try different ways of doing this. Then, ask the children to write their own paragraphs.

Activity 8: How and why KWL chart

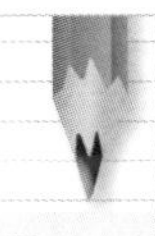

Objective

To adapt non-narrative forms and styles to write factual texts.
(Year 5 Strand 9)

What to do

This activity focuses on what children know, what they want to find out and what they learn, using KWL charts.

- Display an enlarged version of photocopiable page 32. Talk through the column headings with the children, pointing out how the words 'know', 'want' and 'learned' make the initials KWL.
- Thinking of a topic they are learning about, guide the children through the task of filling in the first column by listing what they already know in note form.
- Ask the children what they want to know in the next column. They may ask questions such as: *What is a government?* or *Is the Prime Minister in charge?* However, to prompt explanatory writing, you need to encourage them to ask questions that start with 'how' or 'why', for example: *How are laws decided?* or *Why are there so many MPs?* (Research that stems from these questions will provide suitable material for writing explanations.)
- Follow this up with group work on researching the subject. The children can make notes to answer their questions. Bring the groups together and agree on answers to be recorded in the final column, as well as the children's thoughts about areas that could be explored further.

Activity 9: Pronoun hunt

Objective

To adapt sentence construction to different text-types, purposes and readers. (Year 5 Strand 11)

What's on the CD-ROM

How it works, Encyclopedia entries, and Elections
- Text extracts to read and discuss.

What to do

In this activity, the children look at the way that pronouns often stand in for nouns.

- Ask the children to look at an explanatory text. This could be a copy of an explanation extract from Section 1, but ideally it should be copies of leaflets, magazine or newspaper cuttings that explain something. Ask the children to read the text carefully, looking for pronouns.
- Distribute copies of photocopiable page 33 'Pronoun hunt'. When the children find a sentence with a pronoun they need to cut it out and stick it in the 'snippet of text' section of the photocopiable, making sure they also have the snippet of text that includes the noun to which the pronoun refers. This may be in a different sentence. Ask the children to record the pronoun and noun in the spaces provided.
- Place the children in groups, in which they can share their found pronouns. Because of the way that such texts are structured, the pronouns often refer to an object in a previous sentence as it continues to feature in the process being explained. Encourage the children to think of this as being like the baton in a relay race: the pronoun carries the object forward into the next clause or sentence.
- Ask the children to check whether it is clear what each pronoun refers to. Note any examples of ambiguity on the board, and discuss how they could be rewritten to make them clear.

Activity 10: Jumbled explanations

Objective

To reflect independently and critically on their own writing and edit and improve it. (Year 5 Strand 9)

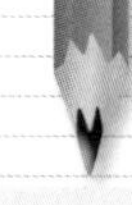

What's on the CD-ROM

Explanation writing
- Roll over the features to reveal examples.

Media resources
- Display and discuss the image 'Teeth'.

What to do

This activity provides a fun way of developing children's understanding of the features that make up and structure an explanation text.

- Revise the main features of explanation writing with the children, emphasising the features presented on the poster on page 18.
- Hand out copies of photocopiable page 34 'Jumbled explanations' – it is obviously jumbled. Point out that there is a common theme of water. As a starting stimulus, display the 'Teeth' image from the CD-ROM.
- Explain that these texts have been jumbled up but three processes are explained. The children need to pick the text apart, separating and sorting the explanations, and put the texts back in order.
- Ask the children as they are doing this, what features they can find that are distinctive traits of an explanation text. They can circle or underline any words that present examples.
- Once this is complete, ask the children to think of other types of texts such as poems, recounts and persuasive texts. Can they list some of the things that distinguish explanatory texts from these other genres?

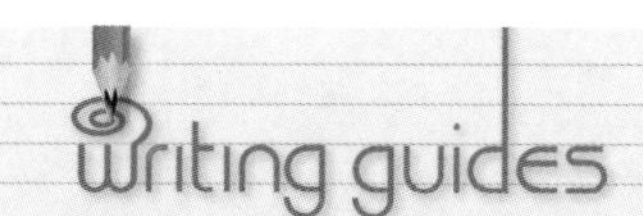

Arrows

- Use this flowchart to plan an explanation text by recording how one stage of a process leads to another.

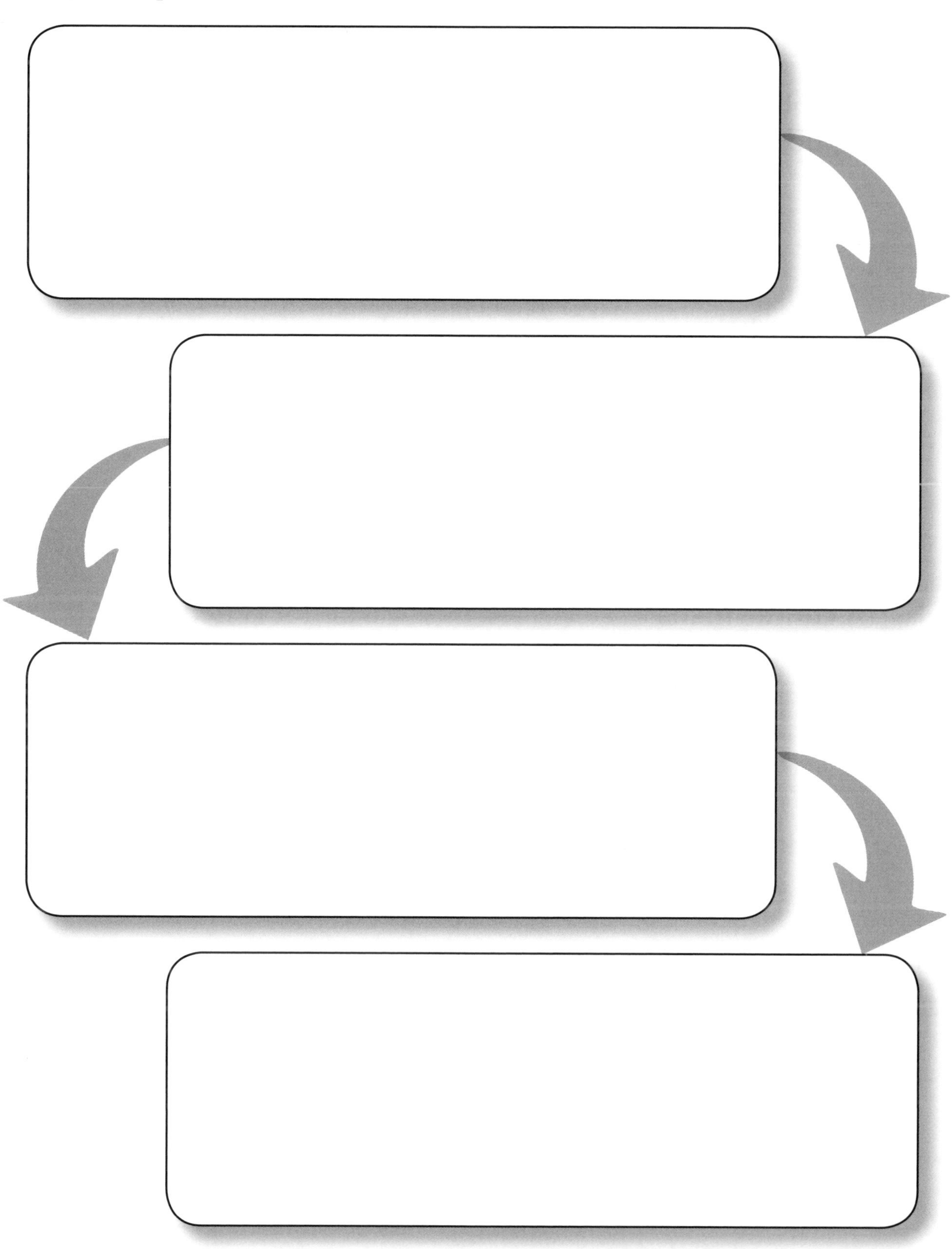

Cause and effect

- Join up the pairs of causes and effects.

The Sun warms a puddle,	because heat from the flame melts the wax.
The particles in a liquid move freely,	because its particles are held strongly together.
A candle melts	when it is heated.
A solid has a fixed shape	so water evaporates more quickly from the surface.
A solid may turn into a liquid	and consequently a liquid has no fixed shape.

Link challenge

- Write two-part sentences using these linking words.

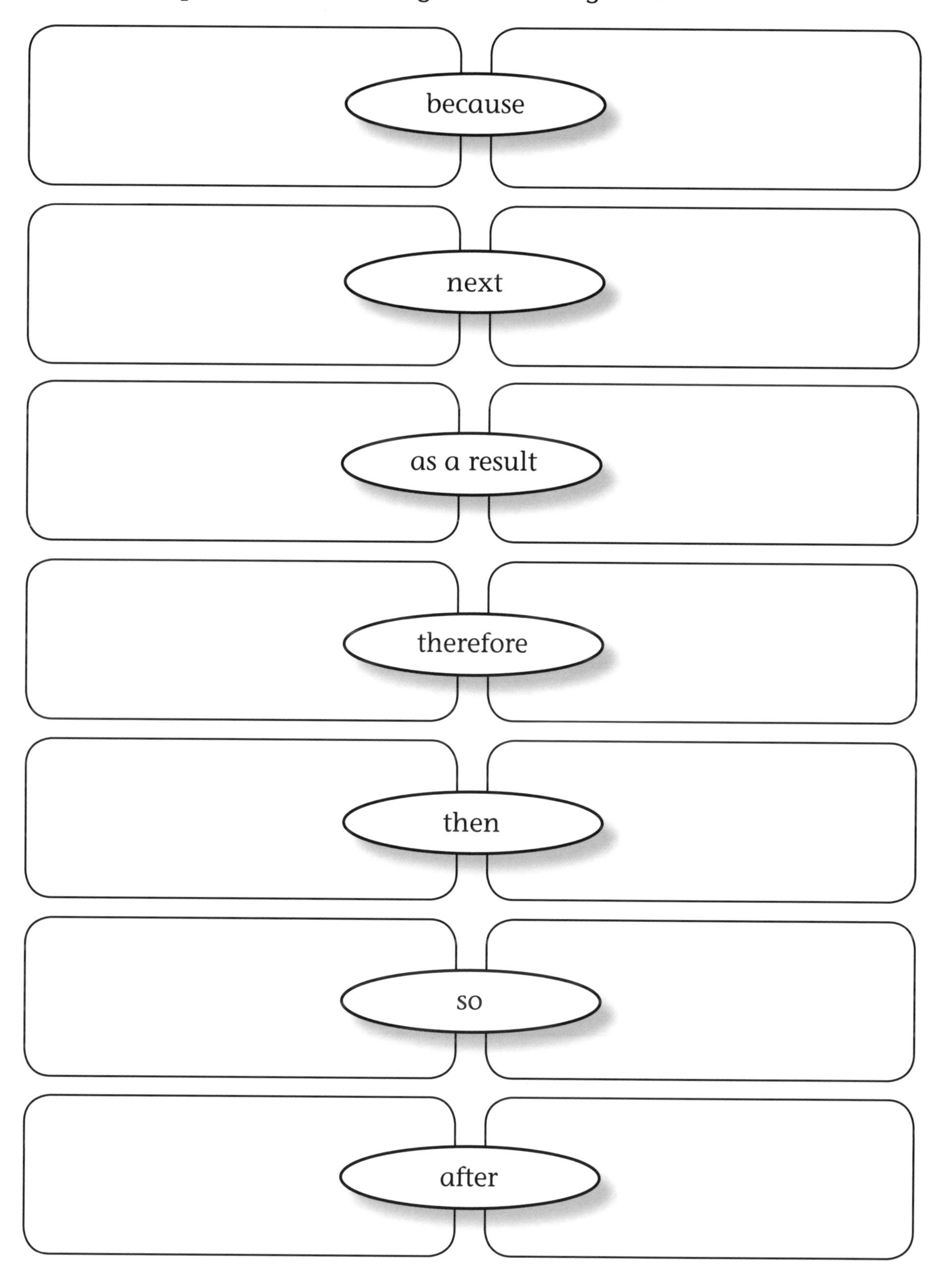

Opening statements

- Complete this table by writing opening statements for explanations.

In an explanation about...	I would answer the question...	An opening sentence could be...

Questioning

- Can you think of two questions to ask about each fact?

The Sun rises in the morning.

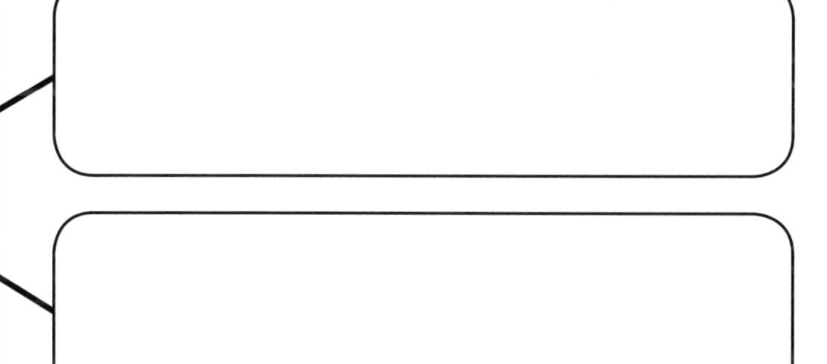

Some birds fly south in the winter.

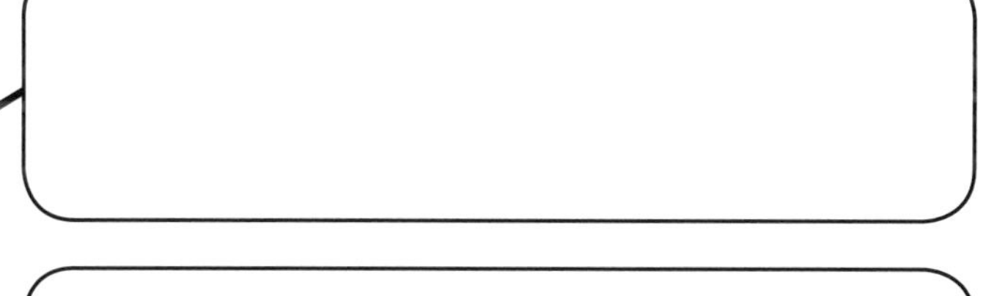

Wax melts when a candle burns.

Cars run out of petrol.

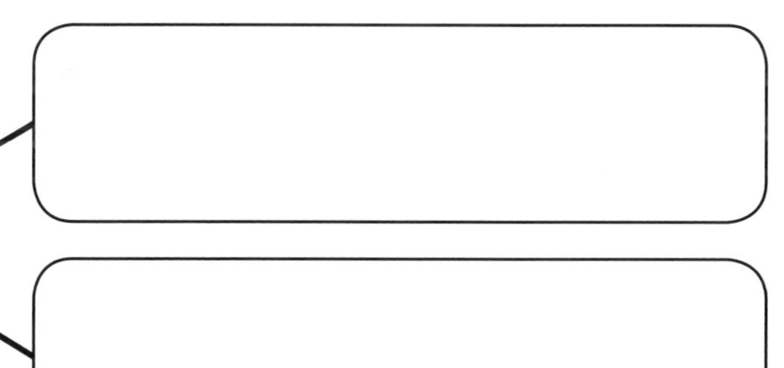

Planning and discussing

- Can you explain these things?

Illustrations © 2003, Andy Miles.

Chocolate changes

- Cut out these sentences and place them in the correct order. Then use them to write an explanation of how chocolate changes when it is first heated and then cooled.

How and why KWL chart

K What we **know**	**W** What we **want** to find out	**L** What we have **learned** or still need to learn

Pronoun hunt

- Find some snippets of text with pronouns and cut them out.
- Stick them in the 'Snippet' space and note down what the pronoun is, and the noun it stands in for.

Snippet of text	Pronoun	Noun

Jumbled explanations

- Cut out these sentences and put them in order.

Our teeth are protected by a hard layer called enamel.
The bigger the surface in contact with the water, the bigger the upthrust.
The water pushes up on the ship with a force called upthrust.
The sea bed interferes with the spiral movement of the water particles, causing the waves to topple over or 'break' on the shore.
Regular brushing keeps plaque off our teeth and so keeps the enamel layer intact.
If the bottom or keel were completely flat, the ship would float even better – but it would be much harder to steer.
Fragments of food caught on them form a sticky coating called plaque in which bacteria can breed – especially when the food contains sugar.
As they approach the shore, the water becomes shallower.
When the decay reaches the nerves in the tooth, the pain starts!

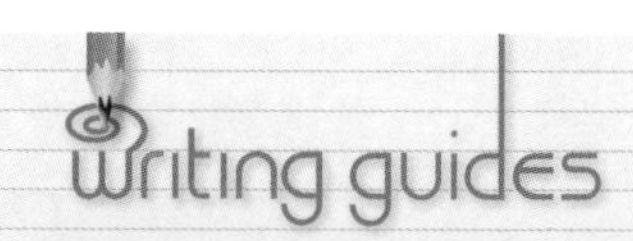

Section 3

Writing

Having built up the skills and components of explanation writing, in this section we apply them to three writing projects. Following the popular notion of scaffolding as a model of good teaching, these three activities gradually remove the support with the aim of children writing their own explanation texts.

The first project takes a common feature of the primary curriculum, the water cycle, and seeks to explain it. The activity also models good explanatory writing, in that it encourages children to shape a variety of resources into the step-by-step process looked at in Section 2 (note, particularly, 'Arrows' on page 20).

The clothes peg activity takes a simple and common object and a process children will readily be aware of, but asks them to write an explanatory text about this. It should be seen as a short set of paragraphs that provide room to polish the structure and language the children are using. It's worth noting that this task is one where you should challenge the children to keep an eye on the poster and ensure they use its guidance throughout their writing.

The final project encourages the children to think of a game with an aim or goal, work out the process to get to the goal and explain it.

These activities all build up to the children researching, questioning and planning their own explanation of a process. As far as possible the children should be let loose to find something they will be interested in. The 'Planning and discussing' activity (on page 22) in Section 2 will build towards this.

The skills used and ideas worked through are all supported by the Section 2 activities that relate to concepts, planning and text structure. All the activities build towards these three projects.

Using the writing templates

The CD-ROM contains four writing templates for the children to use to write their final explanation texts. These can be used on screen, by typing text and inserting images, or you can provide printed versions of these pages for the children to use.

There is a selection of images available in the 'Image bank' that can be incorporated into the writing templates next to appropriate parts of the text. You will also need to show the children how to upload other images into the 'Image bank' by clicking on 'Our images' and 'Add' to navigate to where the image is sorted. A thumbnail picture will be added to the 'My images' gallery.

Writing tips

- Get a good overview of the process you are explaining.
- Chop the process into stages that connect together.
- Figure out what comes when – before and after.
- Ask yourself: how does one thing cause another?
- Use present tense verbs, telling it how it always happens.

Project 1: Water writing

Objective

To adapt non-narrative forms and styles to write factual texts.
(Year 5 Strand 9)

What's on the CD-ROM

Media resources
- Display 'Rain' image.

Water writing
- Roll over text for prompts.

Explanation planner
- Complete a plan.

My explanation text
- Compose a text.

What to do

This activity engages the children in working with notes they gather after collating information about the water cycle from a range of sources.

- Display the image of rainfall on the CD-ROM. Ask the children what they know about the water cycle and make notes.
- Open 'Water writing' from the CD-ROM. Roll over the text, where indicated, to display questions that will prompt discussion of the process and connections across it.
- Hand out copies of photocopiable page 40 and review the notes and refer back to the work on connecting language in Section 2. Then ask the children to explain some of the causes and effects within the cycle. Hand out photocopiable pages 38 and 39 'Explanation planner' (or use the on-screen version) and ask the children to use it to plan an explanation text about the water cycle.
- Refer the children to other reference materials that they have obtained in science or geography work. Point out that it could be useful to refer to these to widen the scope of their knowledge.
- Ask the children to use these notes to produce an explanation text, using the writing templates from the CD-ROM.

Project 2: Clothes peg

Objective

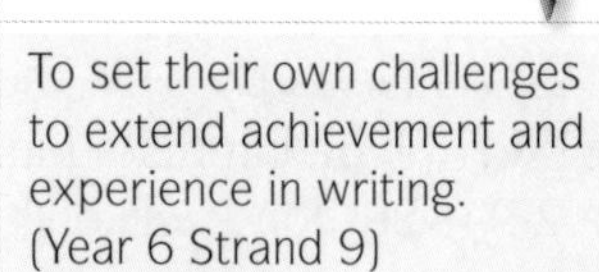

To set their own challenges to extend achievement and experience in writing.
(Year 6 Strand 9)

What's on the CD-ROM

Explanation planner
- Complete a plan.

My explanation text
- Compose an explanation text using the writing templates.

What to do

This activity links with dismantling and explaining technology.

- Before they begin, give each child a clothes peg. Talk about how they work: how simple they are, and yet how useful we find them.
- Ask the class to read the 'Lever' and 'Spring' sections on photocopiable page 41 'Clothes peg', then look at the questions on photocopiable page 42 'Questions about a clothes peg' and make notes for responses.
- Invite the children to complete the diagram at the top of photocopiable page 41 by explaining what each part of a clothes peg does.
- Ask the children to discuss the 'How a clothes peg works' diagrams (page 42) with a partner before cutting out the images and using them as a stimulus for structuring their explanation. They should make notes for an answer to the question 'How do clothes pegs work?'.
- Ask them to consider questions such as: *What is the purpose of the spring? How does the peg exert leverage?* Open the 'Explanation planner' on the CD-ROM or provide copies of photocopiable pages 38 and 39 and encourage them to plan their explanation text.
- Invite the children to write out their explanation text, using the writing templates from the CD-ROM.

Project 3: Game on

Objective

To reflect independently and critically on their own writing and edit and improve it.
(Year 5 Strand 9)

What's on the CD-ROM

Game on
- Text entry activity to plan a process that leads to a goal or aim.

My explanation text
- Compose an explanation text using the writing templates.

What to do

This project takes the idea of a goal or destination, and the process leading up to it, from games. It tackles one of the issues that can trip up explanation writing – the little exceptions and variations on a process.

- Ask the children to give some examples of a goal or an aim in a game. Point out that this can range from being the richest in Monopoly to having attained a level in a computer game. Write a list of the children's suggestions.
- Open 'Game on' from the CD-ROM. Select one of the popular games from the class list, such as football. Discuss with the children what the aim or goal of this game is and type it in the goalpost.
- Next, talk about the process to get to the goal. What has to happen for this to take place? For example, in football, scoring happens following tackling and passing from a kick-off. Work backwards on whatever game you choose and type in the process.
- Ask the children to think of key things that will feature in the process. For example, a football explanation really should, by the time a goal is scored, have mentioned the goal keeper.
- Working in small groups of four or five ask the children to choose one game and to explain the process of it. Try to ensure that the groups are looking at a range of games, and don't simply repeat the shared session.
- Hand out copies of photocopiable page 43 'Game on' for the groups to use. Encourage the children to discuss their chosen game – what are its aims? How do you play? What is the process? Remind the children that they should write the goal in first and work backwards.
- Ask the children to use the photocopiable sheet to draft their explanation. They could use the writing templates on the CD-ROM. Once they have written a draft, encourage them to read it though and check it – is the process clear? The children could work in pairs to do this, commenting on each others' work.

Explanation planner

- Plan your explanation text.

The purpose of this explanation is to answer the question:

Glossary

- What specialist terms will you use? Write their definitions.

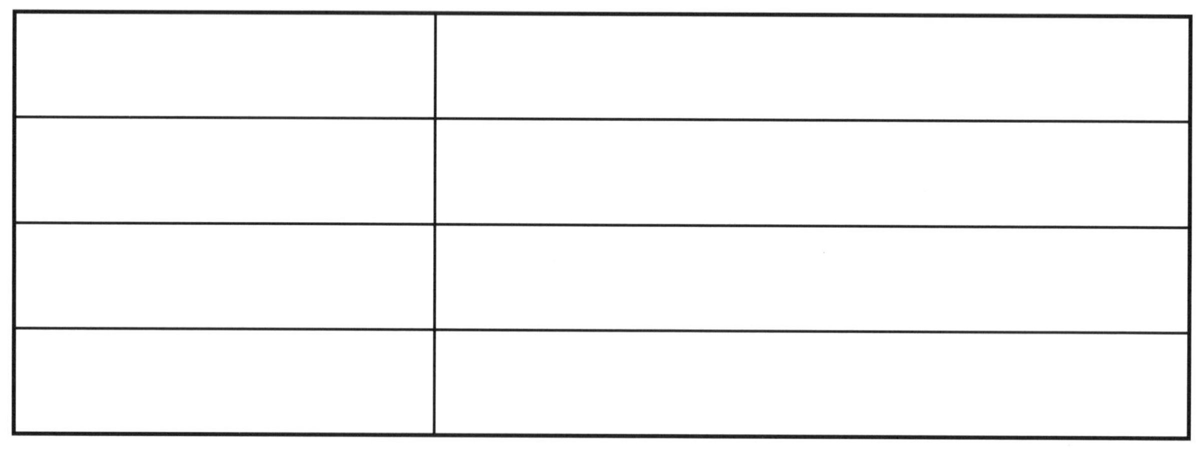

- Write down questions you have about this subject.

Map out the process

- Plot the stages in the process you are explaining by drawing a diagram. Here are three examples:

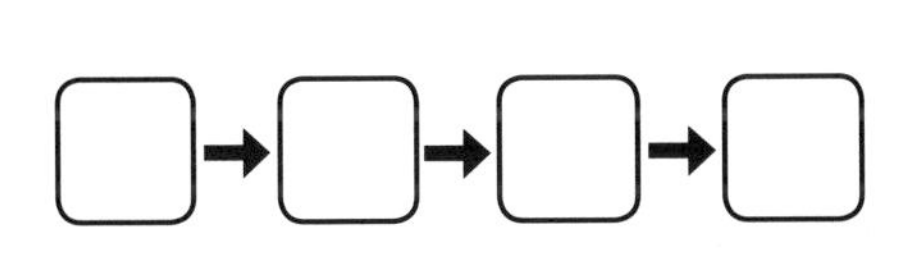
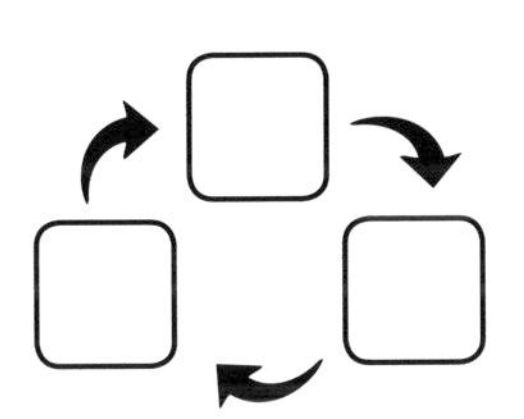
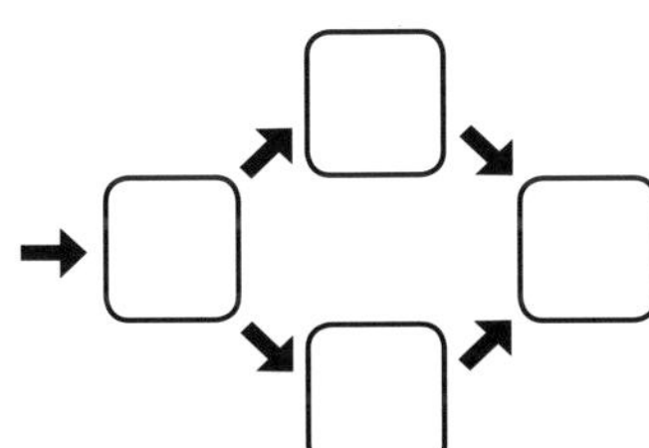

Some key questions

What is being changed?

What is causing the change?

What are the stages in this change?

How does the change start?

How does it end?

Now plan your writing

Opening:

a)

b)

c)

Conclusion:

Water writing

Something you asked a geographer:

How do clouds make rain?

Rain is made by water in a cloud condensing from water vapour to liquid droplets. As the droplets get bigger, they turn into raindrops.

A reminder from your teacher:

Remember!

1. Rivers often flow between mountains.
2. Water is affected by gravity.

Notes from a TV programme you watched:

Water: collects ➜ rivers.
If water goes down through rocks + soil ➜ might join underground stream.

Three extracts from an encyclopedia:

A water molecule can remain in the air for ten days before falling to the ground in a raindrop.

In clouds, small water droplets join together to make bigger drops.

Most rain falls over the sea. When water falls from the sky (as rain, hail, sleet or snow), this is called precipitation.

Something you read on a CD-ROM:

Heat from the Sun causes water to evaporate, turning it into a gas called water vapour. Water vapour rises. The higher it goes the colder it becomes, so it turns back into droplets of water. These droplets form clouds.

Word list on the classroom wall:

Evaporation *Condensation* *Precipitation*

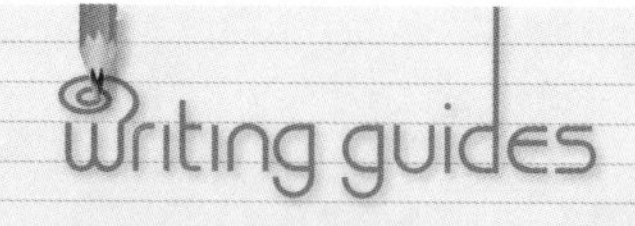

Clothes peg

- What do the different parts of a clothes peg do?

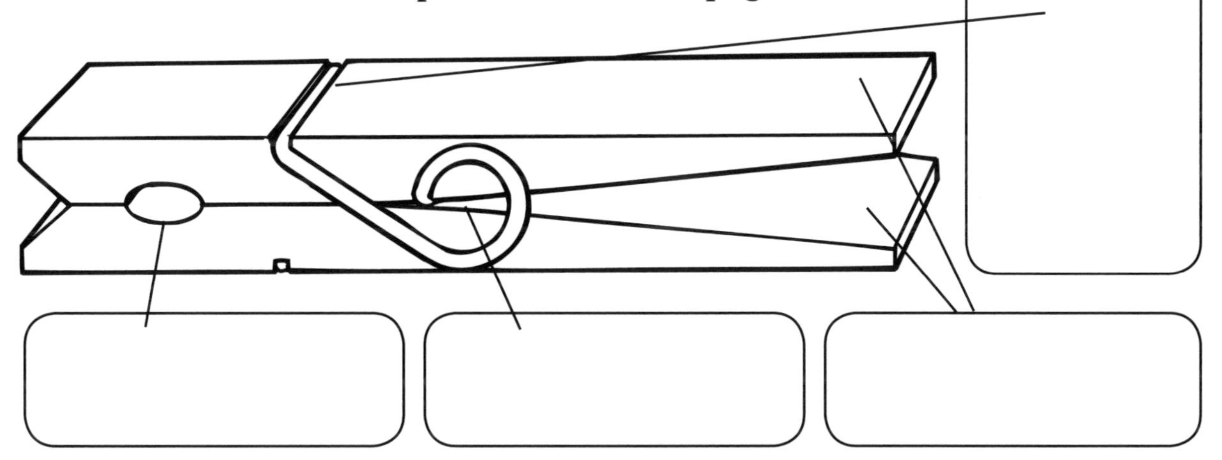

Lever

A lever is a simple machine that makes it easier to move something. It has a load, a fulcrum and an effort.

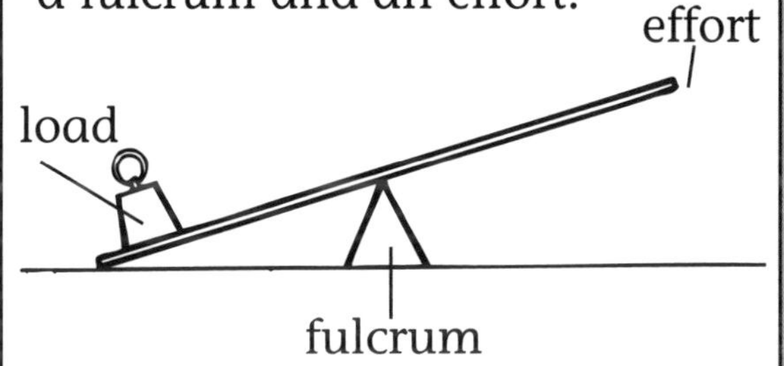

The **fulcrum** is the fixed point around which the lever turns. The **effort** is the force doing the moving. The **load** is the force that has to be moved.

If the arm to which the effort is applied is longer than the arm bearing the load, it is easier to move the load. The longer the effort arm is, the easier it is to move the load.

Spring

A spring is a piece of material, often metal, that is shaped in a particular way.

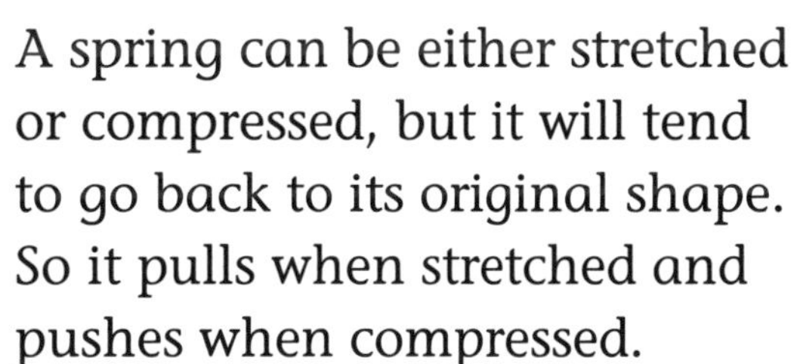

A spring can be either stretched or compressed, but it will tend to go back to its original shape. So it pulls when stretched and pushes when compressed.

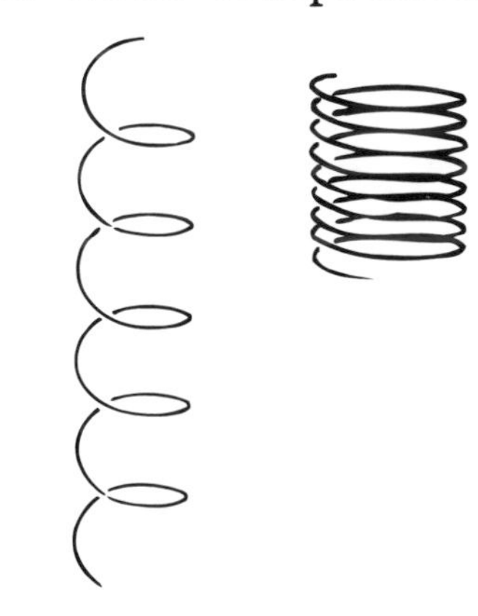

Questions about a clothes peg

- Read and think about these.

What is the load being levered?

Why is the part you pinch so long?

Why is the wood (or plastic) the shape it is?

What are the holes for?

Where is the fulcrum of the lever?

How does the spring connect to the lever?

How a clothes peg works

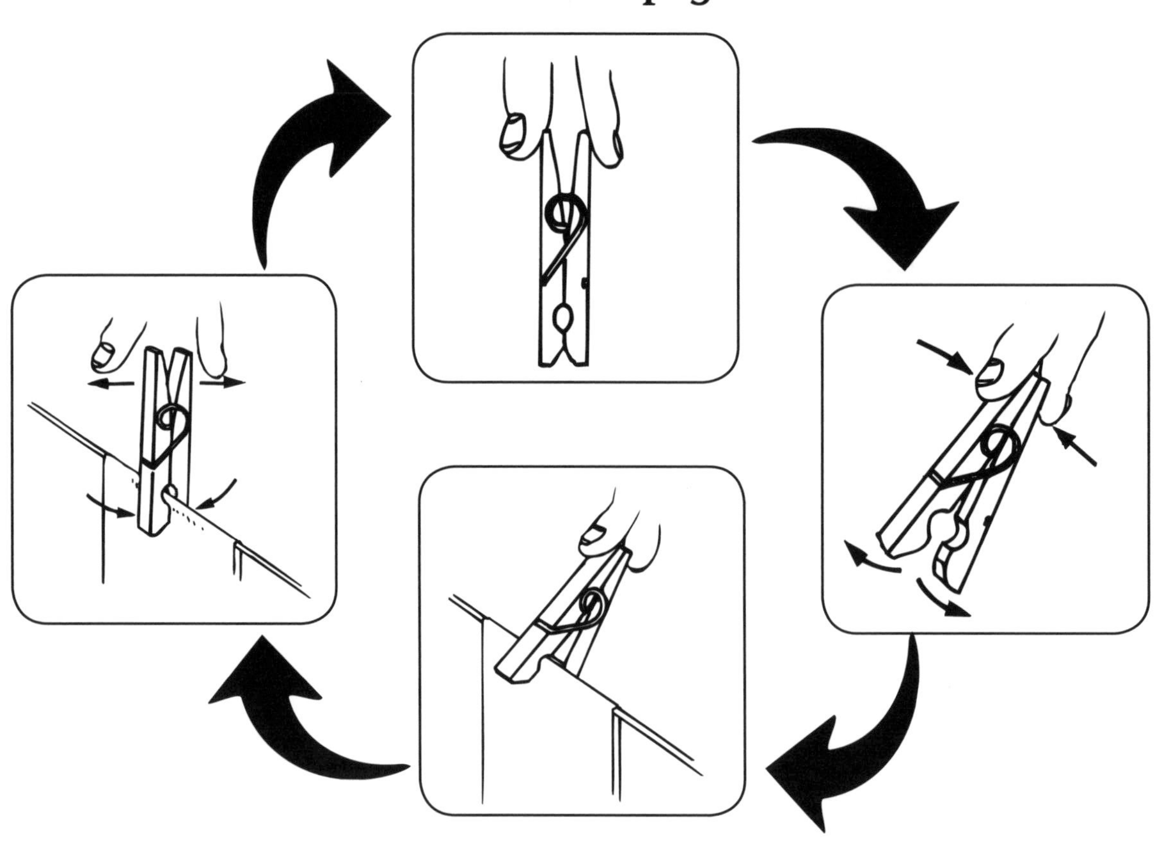

Game on

- Think of a goal for a game and write it in the goalposts. Then think about the process that leads you to that goal. Work backwards to complete the boxes to show the process.

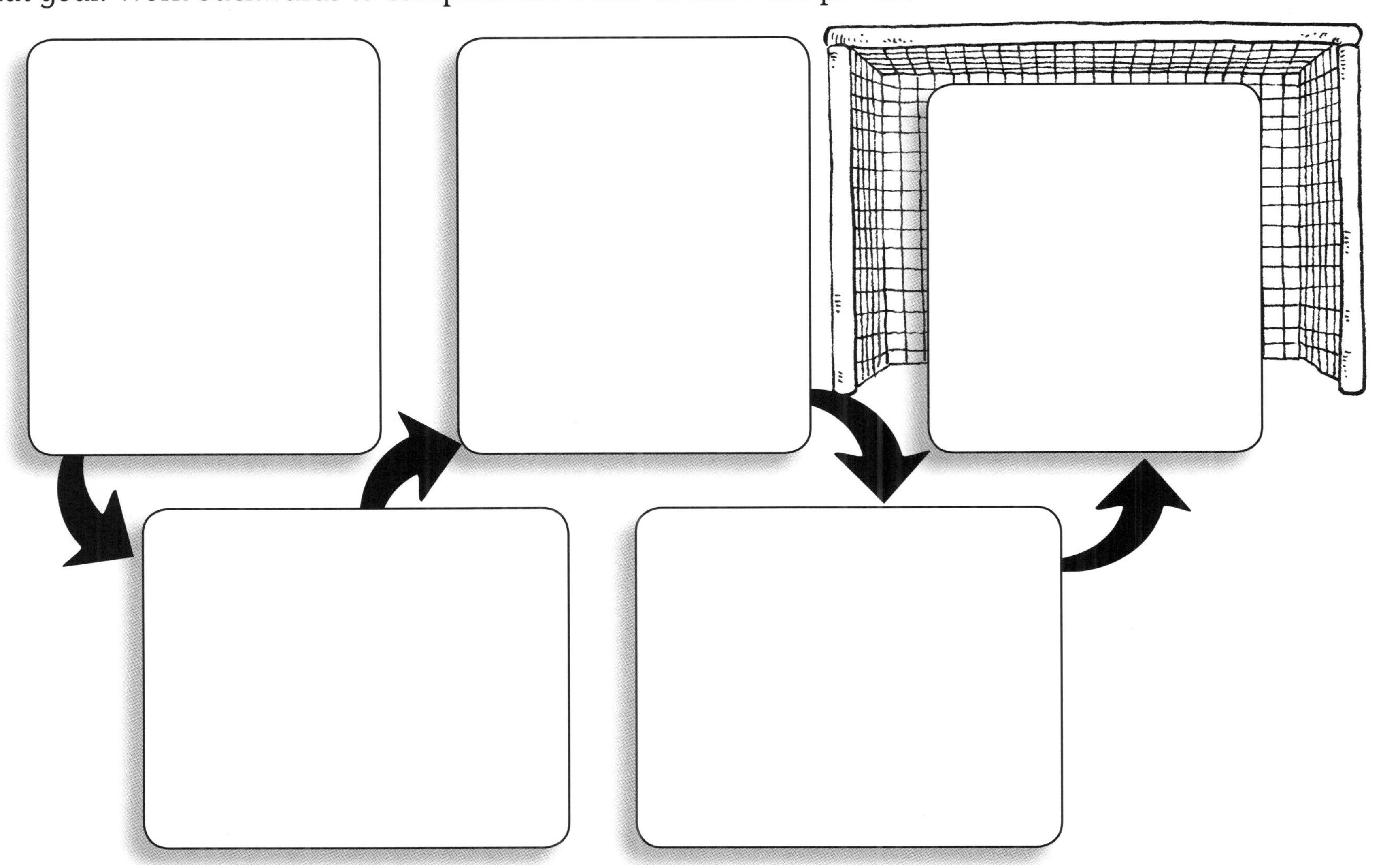

Review

These activities are designed to evaluate how effectively the children have understood the genre and applied the features of it in their writing. By the age of 9–11, they should understand the importance of reflecting on a draft, deciding what can be improved in it and redrafting to produce a final version. These skills can be enhanced by group work in which the children discuss the improvements they could make to their own texts.

Self review

When reading through their explanation, the children should be able to see a clear process being outlined, specialist vocabulary, temporal and/or causal connections, and a change taking place within the process.

A successful explanation should set out to demystify its subject. It should be able to summarise in a phrase or sentence the process or event that is being explained. This is usually outlined in the first sentence, so that the reader is given a clear indication of what the explanation will convey. If it isn't there, adding it might be suggested for a redraft.

The specialist vocabulary used should always be defined somewhere in the text. Again, if it isn't, this can be added in the redraft. The four sections in the checklist will help the children to evaluate their explanations, and aid effective redrafting.

Group review

Working in groups of three, the children should review their explanation writing together. Each child can use photocopiable page 32 'How and why KWL chart' to review all three texts. The sheet encourages the children to consider two specific features of their texts: whether the opening sentence prepares the reader for the rest of the text and what connecting words (causal and/or temporal) they have used. In doing this, children can compare their text with that of the other two children, which makes it easier to identify alterations that they could make to produce a final draft.

Teacher review

What are we looking for? Our two focal review questions in class are: *Why do explanations matter? Why do we read them?*

When reading the children's text you need to consider whether:

- there is an opening statement to identify what is being explained
- it presents a clear process in stages
- things are connected and it shows how one thing leads to another
- connectives are used appropriately and not forced or overused
- the chronology of the explanation is correct
- the use of pronouns is correct
- the use of the present tense is correct and consistent.

Photocopiable page 47 provides the Assessment Focuses for writing to help you assess the children's progress.

Self review

- Read your explanation text and complete this sheet.

What does it explain?

What specialist vocabulary is used?

Can you pick out three stages in the process?

What is changed in this process?

Group review

- Look at the three explanations your group has written.
- Answer these questions for all three pieces of writing.

Which opening sentences did you use?

Which connecting words did you use?

What could you improve in each explanation?

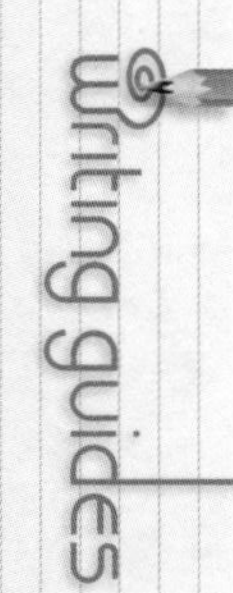

Teacher review

	AF5 **Vary sentences for clarity, purpose and effect.**	AF3 **Organise and present whole texts effectively, sequencing and structuring information, ideas and events.**	AF4 **Construct paragraphs and use cohesion within and between paragraphs.**	AF1 **Write imaginative, interesting and thoughtful texts.**	AF2 **Produce texts which are appropriate to task, reader and purpose.**
LEVEL 4	Some variety in sentences Some varied connectives used in conjoining causes and effects of a process.	Logical sequence of a process explained. Ideas organised with overall introduction and paragraphs that cluster stages in a process.	Paragraphs organise the step-by-step explanation of the process. Limited connectives used between sentences.	Relevant content used in explanation. Some development of details e.g. descriptive language. Viewpoint maintains the focus on the process being explained.	Main purpose specified and guides most writing. Main features of the form – including the step-by-step process – maintained throughout. Clarity of purpose to explain a process clear in the text.
LEVEL 5	Wider range of connectives used to conjoin stages in the process being explained. Sentences structure used to build up detail.	Clear structuring of materials within and across paragraphs. Process is developed through the explanation with clear links between paragraphs.	Paragraphs clearly develop the main flow of the explanation, e.g. clear causal connection Within paragraphs a range of devices support cohesion – explaining a particular step in a process.	Relevant ideas kept throughout the explanation. Ideas developed and shaped across the text. Clarity of focus on the process being explained.	Main purpose specified and undergirds whole text. Features of the selected form adapted to serve the text's purpose.

SCHOLASTIC

Also available in this series:

ISBN 978-1407-11253-4

ISBN 978-1407-11265-7

ISBN 978-1407-11267-1

ISBN 978-1407-11256-5

ISBN 978-1407-11270-1

ISBN 978-1407-11248-0

ISBN 978-1407-11254-1

ISBN 978-1407-11266-4

ISBN 978-1407-11258-9

ISBN 978-1407-11268-8

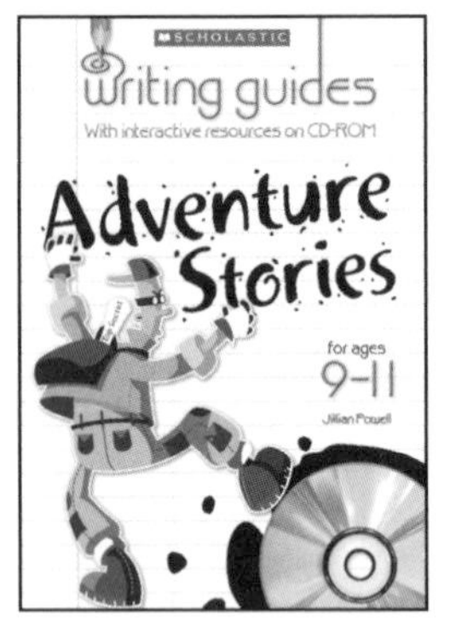

ISBN 978-1407-11251-0

ISBN 978-1407-11257-2

ISBN 978-1407-11255-8

ISBN 978-1407-11269-5

ISBN 978-1407-11250-3

ISBN 978-1407-11247-3

ISBN 978-1407-11252-7

ISBN 978-1407-11264-0

To find out more, call: **0845 603 9091** or visit our website: **www.scholastic.co.uk**